To-Ellie
From—GaG Adel

W9-ART-896

This book belongs to

DeSERENA HONERMAN

One to Grow On™
Bible Series

My Bible ABCs

Written by
Tracy Harrast

Illustrated by
Nancy Munger

ZondervanPublishingHouse
Grand Rapids, Michigan

ONE TO GROW ON SERIES: MY BIBLE ABCs
Copyright © 1998 by The Zondervan Corporation
Text copyright © 1998 by Tracy Harrast

Scripture portions adapted from the HOLY BIBLE, NEW INTERNATIONAL READER'S VERSION™.

Copyright © 1995, 1996, 1998 by International Bible Society.

All rights reserved. No part of this publication may be reproduced, stored in a retrieval system, or transmitted in any form or by any means—electronic, mechanical, photocopy, recording, or any other—except for brief quotations in printed reviews, without the prior permission of the publisher.

Library of Congress Catalog Card Number: 97-61397

Published by Zondervan Publishing House
Grand Rapids, MI 49530, U.S.A.
http://www.zondervan.com
All rights reserved

Author: Tracy Harrast
Illustrator: Nancy Munger
Project Management and Editorial: Catherine DeVries
Interior Design: Sue Vandenberg Koppenol
Art Direction and Cover Direction: Jody Langley

Printed in China

98 99 00 01 02 03 04 /❖HK/ 12 11 10 9 8 7 6 5 4 3 2 1

For Harry & Ruby Leffingwell,
my mom and dad

I remember running home from second grade to
show you my first poem. Your encouragement
led to a life of writing. How can I ever
thank you enough?

A is for angel with news to deliver.

But the angel said to her, "Do not be afraid, Mary. God is very pleased with you. You will become pregnant and give birth to a son. You must name him Jesus" (Luke 1:30–31).

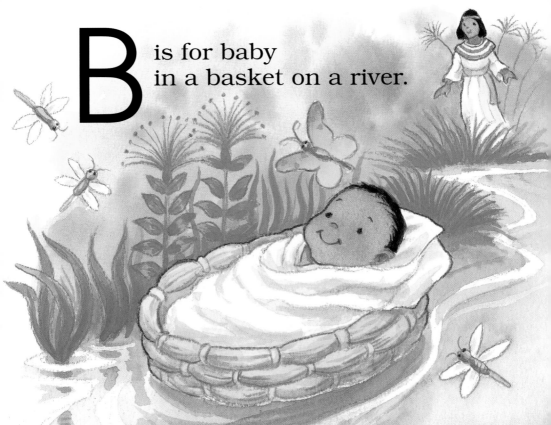

B is for baby in a basket on a river.

[The baby's mother] couldn't hide him any longer. So she got a basket that was made out of the stems of tall grass. She coated it with tar. Then she placed the child in it. She put the basket in the tall grass that grew along the bank of the Nile River. Pharaoh's daughter found the baby. She named him Moses (Exodus 2:3, 10).

C is for children Jesus called to his side.

Jesus said to his disciples, "Let the little children come to me. Don't keep them away. God's kingdom belongs to people like them." Then he took the children in his arms. He put his hands on them and blessed them (Mark 10:14, 16).

D is for donkey that gave him a ride.

Then the disciples brought the colt to Jesus. They threw their coats on the young donkey and put Jesus on it. As he went along, people spread their coats on the road (Luke 19:35–36).

E is for Easter when Jesus left the grave.

The angel said to the women, "Don't be afraid. I know that you are looking for Jesus, who was crucified. He is not here! He has risen, just as he said he would!" (Matthew 28:5–6).

F

is for father who loved and forgave.

"Father, I have sinned against heaven. And I have sinned against you. I am no longer fit to be called your son. Make me like one of your hired workers." His father ... was filled with tender love for his son. He threw his arms around him and kissed him (Luke 15:18–20).

G is for grapes from the promised land.

So the men went up and checked out the land ... The men came to the Valley of Eshcol. There they cut off a branch that had a single bunch of grapes on it. Two of them carried it on a pole between them. They carried some pomegranates and figs along with it (Numbers 13:21, 23).

H

is for houses built on rock and on sand.

Everyone who hears my words and puts them into practice is like a wise man. He builds his house on the rock. But everyone who hears my words and does not put them into practice is like a foolish man. He builds his house on sand (Matthew 7:24, 26).

I is for inn
where travelers stay.

She gave birth to her first baby. It was a boy. She wrapped him in large strips of cloth. Then she placed him in a manger. There was no room for them in the inn (Luke 2:7).

J is for Jesus who takes sins away.

The next day John saw Jesus coming toward him. John said, "Look! The Lamb of God! He takes away the sin of the world!" (John 1:29).

K
is for king who sits on a throne.

King Solomon's throne was decorated with ivory. It was covered with fine gold. The throne had six steps. Its back had a rounded top. The throne had armrests on both sides of the seat. A statue of a lion stood on each side of the throne (1 Kings 10:18–19).

L is for love that our Savior has shown.

No one has greater love than the one who gives his life for his friends (John 15:13).

M

is for manna. Bread from above was delicious.

The people of Israel saw the flakes. They asked each other, "What's that?" Moses said to them, "It's the bread the LORD has given you to eat." The people of Israel called the bread manna. It was white . . . It tasted like wafers that were made with honey (Exodus 16:15, 31).

N

is for net Jesus filled full of fishes.

Jesus said to Simon, "Let the nets down so you can catch some fish." When they had done so, they caught a large number of fish. There were so many that their nets began to break (Luke 5:4, 6).

 **O** is for open your heart's door to Jesus.

Here I am! I stand at the door and knock. If any of you hears my voice and opens the door, I will come in (Revelation 3:20).

P

is for prayer, full of "thank you's" and "please's."

Never stop praying (1 Thessalonians 5:17). *Dear friends, build yourselves up in your most holy faith. Let the Holy Spirit guide and help you when you pray* (Jude 20).

Q

is for quail, food that could fly.

The LORD sent out a wind. It drove quail in from the Red Sea. It brought them down all around the camp. They were about three feet above the ground. They could be seen in every direction as far as a person could walk in a day (Numbers 11:31).

R

is for rainbow
God placed in the sky.

I have put my rainbow in the clouds. It will be the sign of the covenant between me and the earth (Genesis 9:13).

S is for shepherd and sheep that he carried.

Jesus said, "Suppose one of you has 100 sheep and loses one of them. Won't he leave the 99 in the open country? Won't he go and look for the one lost sheep until he finds it? When he finds it, he will joyfully put it on his shoulders" (Luke 15:4–5).

T

is for treasure a man found that was buried.

The kingdom of heaven is like treasure that was hidden in a field. When a man found it, he hid it again. He was very happy. So he went and sold everything he had. And he bought that field (Matthew 13:44).

U is for up. We'll meet Jesus in the air.

We will be taken up in the clouds. We will meet the Lord in the air. And we will be with him forever (1 Thessalonians 4:17).

V is for valley. God's with us even there.

Even though I walk through the darkest valley, I will not be afraid. You are with me. Your shepherd's rod and staff comfort me (Psalm 23:4).

W is for wall written on by a hand.

MENE, MENE

Suddenly the fingers of a human hand appeared. They wrote something on the plaster of the palace wall ... The king watched the hand as it wrote (Daniel 5:5).

X is for exodus through the sea on dry land.

Then Moses reached his hand out over the Red Sea. The LORD ... turned the sea into dry land. The waters were parted. The people of Israel went through the sea on dry ground. There was a wall of water on their right side and on their left (Exodus 14:21–22).

Y

is for "Yes, Lord!" The answer your heart gives.

Jesus said, "I am the resurrection and the life. Anyone who believes in me will live, even if he dies. And those who live and believe in me will never die" (John 11:25–26).

Z

is for Zion. It's heaven, where God lives.

But you have come to Mount Zion. You have come to the Jerusalem in heaven. It is the city of the living God. You have come to a joyful gathering of angels. There are thousands and thousands of them (Hebrews 12:22).

Now that we've read
the alphabet in this book,
can you say it again
without taking a look?